Solastalgia defines an individual's sorrow over climate-change caused losses.

Also by Katerina Fretwell

We Are Malala, (Inanna Publications, 2019)
Dancing on a Pin, (Inanna Publications, 2015)
Class Acts, (Inanna Publications, 2013)
Angelic Scintillations, (Inanna Publications, 2011)
Shaking Hands with the Night, (Pendas Productions, 2004)
Samsara: Canadian in Asia, (Pendas Productions, 2008)
Remyth, (Cranberry Tree Press, 1997) as Kathy Fretwell)
Apple, Worm and All, (Fiddlehead Poetry Books, 1979) as Kathy Tyler.
The Ultimate Contact, (Fiddlehead Poetry Books, 1977).as Kathy Tyler

Holy
in My Nature

Katerina Fretwell

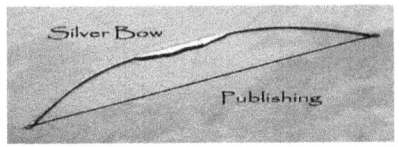

720 – Sixth Street, Box # 5
New Westminster, BC
V3C 3C5   CANADA

Title: Holy in My Nature
Author: Katerina Fretwell
Publisher: Silver Bow Publishing
Cover Art: "Wave" painting by Katerina Fretwell
Layout/Design/Editing: Candice James

All rights reserved including the right to reproduce or translate this book or any portions thereof, in any form without the permission of the publisher. Except for the use of short passages for review purposes, no part of this book may be reproduced, in part or in whole, or transmitted in any form or by any means, either by means electronically or mechanically, including photocopying, recording, or any information or storage retrieval system without prior permission in writing from the publisher.

ISBN: 978-1-77403-290-9 paperback
ISBN: 978-1-77403-291-6 e- book

© Silver Bow Publishing 2024

Library and Archives Canada Cataloguing in Publication

Title: Holy in my nature / Katerina Fretwell.
Names: Fretwell, Kathy, 1944- author.
Identifiers: Canadiana (print) 20240293363 | Canadiana (ebook) 2024029338X | ISBN 9781774032909
   (softcover) | ISBN 9781774032916 (Kindle)
Subjects: LCGFT: Poetry.
Classification: LCC PS8561.R47 H65 2024 | DDC C811/.54—dc23

Holy in My Nature

**to nature lovers,
everyone concerned
about our planetary impact.**

Holy in My Nature

CONTENTS

SECTION I: UNNATURAL ANTHROPOCENE.

Holy in My Nature / 11
Weapons of Mass Revelation / 12
The View from Above, Housing Who / 13
Personal Anthropocene / 14
Eulogy / 15
Mindful Burn, Nairobi / 16
Hambach Mine / 17
Potash Mine #2 / 18
Dandora Landfill / 19
Clear-cuts and Cut-blocks / 20
Cararra Marble / 21
Lagos, Nigeria, Malthusian Growth / 22
Imperial Valley #4 and 5, California / 23
Tetrapods and Technofossils / 24
Phosphate Mining, Lakeland, Florida / 25
Fracking, Mining, Transporting / 26
Micro Burst Plastics Primer / 27
A (Re)Use for Everything / 28

SECTION II: NATURAL REMEDIES, NATURAL PLAGUES?

Trashing Plastic – Longevity / 31
Trashing Plastic - Saving Shifting Sands / 32
Trashing Plastic – Saltwater Light / 33
Forests Primeval / 34
Primal Peace / 35
Floral Consolation / 36
Public and Private Gardens / 37
Anthem / 38
Peter Pan's Lost Boys and Girls / 39
The Profit-Line Becomes the Priest / 40
Allegiance / 41
Watery Dirge / 42
Greta Thunberg / 43
Covid Correction / 44

SECTION III: HOLY IN MY NATURE

Ode to Parry Sound / 47
Anatomy of a Wave / 48
Cellular / 49
Water Sign / 50
Spindrift / 51
Unbroken / 52
South Pacific and Mid-Atlantic / 53
Out of the Woods Yet / 54
Death By Google / 55
To My Daughter / 56
It's No Hoax / 57
Natural Divinity / 58
Scaling Down / 59
Harmony / 60
Solitude / 61
Fledging / 62
Expansion / 63
Naming / 64
To Be a Bay / 65
Henry's Guests / 66
Labyrinth / 67
Blessings for my Grandchild / 68
Nature Sings, Listen / 69
Burning Up #1 To Fossil Fuellers / 70
Burning Up #2 Can We Put the Fire Out / 71
Burning Up #3 Combustible Legacy / 72
Burning Up #4 Don't Bet on It / 73
Burning Up #5 Wild Prayer / 74
Burning Up #6 Our Grievous Embrace / 75
Burning Up #7 Why Do Whales Wail / 76
Burning Up #8 Fiery Pyre / 77
Honourable Harvest / 78

Testimonials / 79
ENDNOTES / 80
Acknowledgements / 81
Author Profile / 82

SECTION I:

UNNATURAL ANTHROPOCENE.

Holy in My Nature

Holy in My Nature

My heart beats louder than my head
when climate news smacks the airwaves.
Predictions propel me to squall. The sky is falling –
beloved Boreal forests – ablaze, bombarded, gone!

The science eludes me; the science can save us.
But – escaping Chemistry and Physics,
I inched through Biology.
In Bio 101, the prof bared his torso
to demo muscles in action.

My cerebrum muscled overtime,
digesting osmosis and evolution between acting
the lead in the satire, *School for Scandal*.
Named the foetal pig I dissected – for the prof.

But I can't depart from the climate-crisis beat.
The evidence is indisputable:
In 2018, my deep-drilled well dried up.
In 2023, hottest recorded year to date, whole towns,
Canada's forest canopy, cougars and crops, crackled, vanished.

The AGO's Anthropocene Show burned
human desecration of Earth's well-being
into visual shocks – condo-sized machines,
town-large landfills, quarries seen from space ...

Lifelong forest lover,
I'm bathed in peace; woodlands the world over
hold my hand, mother me
out of the Ferris wheel of fortune,
mine and others.
My head echoes my heart,
urging me in holiness:
act, hope, kneel, pray.

Weapons of Mass Revelation
Edward Burtynsky, Jennifer Baichwal, Nicholas de Pencier, Anthropocene (2018).

There I stand, stilled, silenced, sepulchral,
gazing not only at a photo show at the AGO,

but also, at a cathedral of sarcophagi –
each mural or film still,
digitally stitched like an electronic quilting bee,
unflinchingly mirrors
the fast track of our human impact.

I bow before this uncanny altar
lit up in rhino horns, gouged earth, steaming rivers,
toxic tailing, smog trails, barren bluffs.

How on earth did the author/photographers
risk their lives by slapping lenses
high onto choppers, low onto diving bells …
to poke inside mountains, seafloors,
sinkholes swallowing family homes,
oil refinery islands stinking waterways?

Drones increasing their reach,
the trio presents this final frontier –
eroding and exploding, frying and dying
as we elbow space, prod soil, stifle rivers,
shoot for fun, eat all we see, grow our garbage …
not to grind us in guilt, but to goad us
into stewarding that which sustains us:
trees to breathe, soil to flower, water to float life.

The View from Above, Housing Who
The usefulness of aerial views is that the viewer ... move(s) from the unfamiliar to the familiar. ~ Anthropocene, 16.

Interchangeable streets and split-levels
portrayed my Seventies enclave:
each sprouting a sapling welcome mat –
which is my street, my house.
Is this a Tinker Toy Town on repeat?

In the sprawling Postwar Dream,
Mom and I bowed down to the TV altar –
Madison Avenue's endless ads:
Frigidaire, coal chute, wringer-washer ...
telling fox, lynx, and bear to get lost,
bulldozing their homes to kingdom come.
I didn't spare them a thought;
neither did the media.

Our continental breadbasket
succumbed to slums and barrens,
hastened by copious combustion, cheap construction,
drive-in movies in heated comfort, toasty garages, gas-lit hearths ...
oblivious to hit men, Fossil Fuel and Almighty Cement.

Let's re-theme the North American Dream.

Personal Anthropocene
Through reciprocity the gift is replenished. All of our flourishing is mutual. ~ Robin Wall Kimmerer, Braiding Sweetgrass, (2013),166.

Solastalgia defines an individual's sorrow
over climate-change caused losses.

Near Parry Sound, where I lived for 40 years,
I mourned the dropped populations:
fox, moose, bear, beaver, turtle,
woods walks and swims empty as a cemetery.

I tallied barberries crowding out wintergreen,
zebra mussels muscling out pickerel and pike.

Come Spring, I emptied the patch of ramps,
until swept into an attitude of gratitude,
respect for this unsolicited bounty,
and horror at the colossal carbon cost
of my longing for leeks in winter.

No sense preening at the epoch
named for mankind.
My footprint reflects the oversized ego
that deems people queen of all species,
a phrase refracting my rare but unstoppable
bouts of shopping,
mainly for bargains and books,
shelves and closets overflowing.

Eulogy
all five species of rhinoceros have been brought to the edge of extinction because of demand for their distinctive horns. ~ Anthropocene, 2018, 178.

("Baby Elephant Walk" music from Hatari, 1962, Henry Mancini, plays softly)

As Director of Sapiens Funeral Homes, I have grievous news –
I must sadly impart that Sudan passed into glory
      --20 March, 2018--
Kenya's last male white rhino,
survived by two females.
Please donate to Save the Rhino and Tusk Trust.

Do not call our funeral home chain, we're deluged
by the growing ghost parade:
tusks, hides, tails, claws and paws ...
Sure, cute dead mammals raise the most grief,
but, Pisces lovers, forget salmon sushi,
fish are hardest hit!

Dear mourners, do note:
rhino horns cure nothing;
and rhino balls don't engorge you
to rise to the occasion.

Join us post-service for barbecued rhino rib.

Mindful Burn, Nairobi, Kenya, 2016

President (Kenyatta's) Pile ... would make a bold statement that there is no market for ivory. ~ Anthropocene, 180.

My eyes whizzed over hillocks – stitched-stills
flashing six thousand elephants' ivory tusks,
up in smoke to deter poaching
for quick bucks and my colonial trinket-lust.

Stacked like a twenty-foot tiara,
the tusk pyre burns thievery and coveting,
such as the ivory bookends
my parents acquired a while ago.

Schooled as a consumer, I had to erase
a compulsion for booze and beer.
When first sober, I unchained my six-packs,
ceded the stash.

Let all mammals roam.

Let me treasure gestures over things –
the lope, not the trophy;
the pounce, not the ground round;
the wildlife photo, not the ivory pendant
or bookends.

Hambach Mine
Lignite is a particularly inefficient and dirty fuel ... Germany still leads the EU in carbon emissions as of 2017. ~ Anthropocene, 122.

What's it like to steer a Bagger,
the biggest machine in human history?

Stifled inside the cab, I'd quake
at its shrieking, growling earthquake
huge as two conjoined-condos!

Mechanical Superman's 18-bucket wheel
lops mountaintops and crushes trees
       in a single swipe,
creating man-made hills that smother
wildflowers, dwellings, businesses, towns.

Sure, Superman makes a bundle,
but what of family and friends
fleeing depleted lignite and evicted villages?

Superman, The Hulk, The Joker
are here to stay, we clone
bigger, better Baggers globally.

Potash Mine #2

Five mines operate in and around the city of Berezniki, ... an estimated ten thousand kilometres of tunnels. As a result, ... Berezniki (Russia) has experienced giant sinkholes. ~ Anthropocene,142.

The mural's extracted-potash glows
red, ochre and sienna spirals
entrancing as ammonites.
But what an unholy web,
a black widow army of tunnels.

Only recently, I clued into potash fertilizing my food,
factory farms fast-forwarding greens, seafood ...
        that I still buy.

What if I married a miner in Berezniki?
Picture stewing Sunday supper,
singing to my sweetheart on a sofa,
or chilling with a book,
or posting wages on the Web –
when BOOM! we disappear,
our home sucked into a gigantic hole –
tunnelled, no trace – as if we never lived ...
earth a lacy winding-sheet.

I was only reading Dante,
not dreaming I'd live the Inferno,
die in one of the subterranean rings.

Dandora Landfill
... is *among the largest of its kind in the world.* ~ *Anthropocene*, 62.

On tour in '93, my stunned eyes shut out families
squatting on the Lecithin landfill.

Today, it's agony to absorb Dandora's filmed roads
ringing a garbage city two stories high!

Our Pandora's Box of Western waste:
tires, wires, laptops, food-wraps, tractors, vials –
feeds you, Nairobi's poor, dumpster-diving

       Golden Globe of Toxic.

You resell this grim reap to reuse,
as cancers suffuse you and your kin –
there's no other route to feed, clothe,
       shelter loved ones.

Clear-cuts and Cut-blocks
British Columbia['s] rainforest occupies only 10 percent of Canada's area, yet.
contains (most) of (its) vertebrates, plants (and) bird and mammal species.
~ Anthropocene, 166.

On a visit, I kneel to Stanley Park's Seven Sisters
that withstood 2008's toppling gales.
This cathedral of trees reminds me
the world is not mine to bend at will.

How much old growth remains virginal?
Even this slice stands in Big Logging's sites –
chainsaws invading centuries,
molesting millennial-aged cedars.

      His brethren felled,
Big Lonely Douglas Fir waves in vacant space,
saved by an ex-logger reborn as a saviour of trees.

Her twins, snug in a double stroller, my stepdaughter
and I gaze into the clouds, enthralled
by these finite Titans, worth more uncut,
ascending into the infinite.

Carrara Marble
... quarries operating at this scale leave [their] lasting trace upon our planet ...
~ Anthropocene, 148.

I stretch my neck up, up, up – no horizon,
the Carrara wall fills the picture plane.

A quarry-man claims the total taken
"Is just a pig's plucked hair."

But such quarries, worldwide, I recall
after climbing China's Great Wall,
      poke their noses,
in the sights of satellites in space.

Bathing my tour-bleary eyes in '96
on Michelangelo's *David,*
I flinched at the locals' glare:
taxed to keep treasures intact,
their factories clone *David* into tourist trifles
      that I bought into.

Lagos, Nigeria, Malthusian Growth
One of the economic capitals of Western Africa, [Lagos is a] series of islands and peninsulas ... at a high risk of flooding. ~ Anthropocene, 72.

In my biased Western eyes, I was clueless
that Lagos is the world's fastest growing city,
their millions projected to shove USA numbers
into the dust in half a century,
like a Lamborghini: zero to fifty in six.

Straddling surge and erosion,
stilt-dwellers shudder at the wall
proposed to protect the rich tech sector,
       redirecting floodwaters
          onto their shaky frames?

And what of white Western car and cow farts
causing climate carnage that floods and fries
those same not-consulted people?

Comfortable carbonate that I am,
my small restitution: Gifts of Hope
help so few of the destitute survive
our hapless humanity.

       It is a race ...
one gift, one life; one gift, one life ...
     a billion times over.

Imperial Valley #4 and 5, California
... farmers, who use 85 percent of Colorado's water supply, struggle to change their practice. ~ Anthropocene, 88.

Farms the size of the stagnant Salton Sea
stream billions in profits for greens –
the same I munch each lunchtime –
via siphoning off the Colorado,
sole water source of this Hades-hot valley.

Sucker-punched by this arid reveal,
Jennifer Baichwal photographed our tainted trail,
blazing "Anthropocene" onto viewers' lips.

Digitally split off from nature,
we Westerners witness higher hell-fires
setting the West Coast alight,
sucking scarce water from fighting the flames.

How long can these farmers supply my salads,
    how long can they feed our families
before we're dumped into the dustbin of history?

Tetrapods and Technofossils
... *serve as future geologic markers.* ~ *Anthropocene, 68.*

What if rising oceans jet-spray into nonexistence
my birthplace, New York, or education-site, Halifax?
A billion people cling to coastlines.

Katrina smashed New Orleans into a sandcastle,
mostly poor Black Ward Nine: dead underwater.

Cooked into concrete, sand's our prime Lego set.
China's concrete seawalls, called Tetrapods,
try to stop surging tides
like a dinky finger stoppering a dike.

Over decades, I've stood by while developers'
unstoppable tarmac paves over
flood-plain, wetland, arable loam,
becoming the new billboards,
like flysch or tree rings
marking humanity's geologic graffiti.

Phosphate Mining, Lakeland, Florida
... beyond a population of 7.8 billion, agricultural land ... (needs) to be significantly more productive. ~ Sir George Knibbs, The Shadow of the World's Future (1928), quoted in Anthropocene, 116.

In the Twenties, Sir George echoed Malthus:
we humans are outgrowing our food supply –
and we pour phosphate onto farmland
that bolsters growth, but poisons
soil and sod, salmon and sea, through its residue –
like chemo kills our loved ones to cure their cancer.

Where our food sources go, we go.
Yes, we all die – but all at once?
Since the Seventies, three-fourths of all species
have followed the dinosaur –
yet disappeared under my radar!

Now their Great Dying haunts me.
How do I green my bond with food?

Will looking on all lifeforms
as my brothers and sisters save me?
I picture our planet – post-people, thriving.

T-Rex ruled the dinosaurs.
We humans think we're a gift.

Nature, molested by our species,
has other ideas.

Fracking, Mining, Transporting
... until a more efficient form of energy is found, global sustainability will take a back seat to the status quo. ~ Anthropocene, 128.

Humanity's the foremost thief –
we steal species' habitats and herds,
stillbirth tree and sea;
allies that help us breathe.

The thief, fracking, cracks rocks into fissures,
sacrificing tons of sand and water.

Mining aborts the earth's fertility,
like seines striptease the oceans for one species,
say the lobster I crave –
while precious others rot, for no reason.

Now we've broken a record
held since Earth was birthed –
doubling our carbon-to-oxygen ratio
in one century.

Weaned on capitalism's *Me First,*
when will we lift our heads,
hidden in time's ghostly sands?

Micro Burst – Plastics Primer

Who knew that plastics, even invisible particulates,
permeate every area of life?

Who knew that micro-plastics shape-shift
to prey their way into long life?

Who knew, that, shed in clothes-washers,
microfibers leach onto my food, water. Skin?!

That, canoodling in my toothpaste and towels,
micro-beads sleep rough in water treatment plants.

That, zapped airborne by UV rays, plastic-fragments
muscle into wildlife guts and sweat PCBs.

That, frequent flyers, heat-slimmed nurdles,
hitch rides in our breaths.

That warmed Styrofoam taints the food it contains,
swaggers into all things marine.

That I'd do well, after maligning the Fifties,
to adopt its make-it-last and make-it-do mindset.

A (Re)Use for Everything

Three cheers for eccentricity:
watching worms turn leftovers into fertilizer,
Tom Szaky grew the process into TerraCycle.

Invented user-friendly reusable wraps,
turned one-off waste
that share the same polymer structure
into usable items:
bags into bowls, cigarette butts into benches ...
and proved zero junk is doable.

But not done.

So, he made recycle reuse easy:
No bother. No money-grab. No tedious time.
The shortest road to re-birthing us green.

If sickos can let go of tainting Tylenol,
thus companies can let go of thrice-wrapping
to prevent lawsuits over poisoned products.

If we consumers can ignore goods wrapped in paranoia ...
we may stand a chance.

Section II:

Natural Remedies, Natural Plagues?

Holy in My Nature

TRASHING PLASTIC

Longevity

Distraught over global food shortages and starvation,
James Rogers designed edible skins
protecting produce
that keep water, sweat less, stay decay,
and energize the eater,
graciously vanishing,
unlike Styrofoam and Saran wrap.

Could less wasted plant parts expiate
the mortal sin of global famine?

If we, who are well fed,
foment for fair access and stop Big Food
from curbing supply to place profits
over people's well-being,
we'd sever forever that cruelly unjust
distribution system:
the bondage of food-wrapped-in-politics.

TRASHING PLASTIC

Saving Shifting Sands

What a wish: The chance to swim with sea turtles
as I did eons ago from a Hawaiian public beach.

Now, condos, roads ... a cacophony of concrete
covers the overcrowded globe,
binges on sand as if infinite.

And hurricanes strip resorts and public beaches alike.

But a New Zealand brewery blasts
used beer bottles into sand-like particles in seconds,
using only the minute portion of energy required
to break down the glass.

Employed widely – no bottled landfills,
no bottle-neck transport, no concrete contrails.

      What a wish:
Only acres of mellow sand, renewed reefs ...
that oasis restorative as forest bathing.

TRASHING PLASTIC

Saltwater Light

Imagine a plug-free light shining for six months.

Aisa Mijeno invented the Salt Lamp –
one tablespoon of salt to one cup of water
halos eight hours of light,
cheap and easy
to brighten islanders' lives.

She convinced kerosene users to renounce
its health-robbing, climate-boiling toxins.

Surely Mother Earth exhales in relief
when we use what's safe and freely accessible,
without gouging her for the rare and ruinous
unholy substances.

Forests Primeval

Sunnybrook Hospital's oak stand soothed me
during a weight loss program.
Later the grove lost out to the Brain Science building.

Heroes, Florence Nightingale and Qing Li,
    proved: trees are good medicine.

In Seguin, shinrin yoku, Japanese for forest bathing,
washed my eyes in wildflowers and wintergreen,
purging a dumpster's worth of facts and to-do lists
that vamoosed among Buglos and Birdsfoot,
       mullein and mayflower.

Whether grieving kin's distance or chasing choral notes,
I slid inside stands of giant pines and frothy ferns,
recouping my youthful shape.

Better yet, Sunnybrook displays a new grove
       to soothe patients
       and having moved,
   I can walk to my daughter's house.

Primal Peace
The Boreal Forest is the only inheritance of every living child born today because it is our environment. ~ Diana Beresford-Kroeger, *Arboretum Borealis: A Lifeline of the Planet (2010), 1.*

Old growth, Boreal, Carolinian, rain-forest,
constant friends, I hugged you as a homing, a baptism.

Changeling gusts of newly met birch, beech, balsam...
       whoosh through life as I lived it:
         having transformed
  character, careers, family, friends, homes.

Despite blight and broken branches,
my forest trees anchored me
like nurse logs leavening sprouts.

Roots commune through fungal weave.

Woodpeckers bored boles that nestled squirrels,
dimpled light narrated nutrients,
songbirds serenaded me.

Nature whispers, clicks, and booms
for all remaining forests – our global gift.

In my new city apartment far from woodlands,
I still wonder why we humans squander our heirloom
As if chopping up inherited antiques.

Floral Consolation
"Earth laughs in flowers" ~ Ralph Waldo Emerson

My artist aunt christened our cottage
with congregant daffodils and dahlias,
defusing drunken grownup spats and cousin splats.

My father's friend consoled us with white roses
after Daddy died at 38.

Mom's gardener, a World War II Italian refugee,
graced our home with morning glories
and boxed spruce which I climbed down
when banished to my bedroom for backtalk:
Why does God have us in His sites?

Shortly after, both parents deceased,
I wept to my prep-school prom date;
he pinned an orchid corsage over my heart.

Now I'm widowed, but well-loved and flower-blessed;
geraniums anoint my kitchen and balcony.

After cut iris' fleeting bliss, I feast on
    a field of divine dandelions.

Yet these songs of sunlight are dismissed
    as throwaway weeds.

Private and Public Gardens
However, divided we may feel within ourselves, it is the sum total of our warring fractions that makes us who we are – fragmentary but indivisible. ~ Maria Popova, Figuring (2020), 154.

Scanning my lifespan, yes,
I've dead-headed my share of rose-beds.
Prickled by nettle-slurs, thorny, faith bled out.
I failed to divert poison sumac attacking my daughter,
later labelled my grandchild's funk, belladonna blue.

Blighted, wilted – as insights slowly taprooted,
I've uprooted rotten thinking
and transplanted forlorn graces
into healthier humus, healing gardens.

Global gardens, glysphosphate-gilded,
      dry, flood or fry.
Raise me up to revere, restore
and rotate heirloom crops,
blemished but diverse, I can still grow whole.

Anthem
If you truly love nature, you will find beauty everywhere. ~ Vincent Van Gogh

Listening, standing witness, creates an openness to the world in which the boundaries between us can dissolve in a raindrop. ~ Braiding Sweetgrass, 300. (Seguin Township April, 1982 – April, 2023)

Swirling grain of weathered nurse-log,
    denuded pine rising from wetlands,
        field of daisies, buttercups, irises,
            indigo bunting homing teal rays.

            Patterned quilt of autumnal leaves,
        road's swath through crimson, gold,
    wintergreen berries breathing cooler air,
squirrels playing tag up and down the oak.

Sky blindingly cobalt at high noon,
    snow crystals chorusing in prisms,
        beech bravely bearing sunlit leaves,
            rabbit, partridge here, now hidden.

            Trillium herald the snow's recession,
        corn goddess and god thirstily kissing,
    black leaves sway under swamp surface,
woodpeckers drumming ironwood in sync.

Birth, growth, decay, death procession,
    seasoned holy, embodies my stages,
        presenting before my awakened eyes:
            eye-wide, gratitude no mere platitude.

            Sun dimpling, snow smoothing,
        lightning revealing, how can I not
    revere these pageants inviting witness:
preserve every imperilled speck and act.

Peter Pan's Lost Boys and Girls
He who wants a rose, must respect the thorn. ~ Persian proverb

Trash-talk reduces self-love to a flashed emoji:
girls hoard *Likes*, doomed to *Never-land*
if the tally's below a thousand fans.

High on street drugs, gangs walk the plank,
start random fires, spray-paint a pool,
defacing lilies, lands and lodges – to be *Cool*.

Slaving long hours with no helpmates,
latchkey children's solo moms, Wendys,
lack the village required to love one or many.

No communal woods walks, birding,
track and field sports, even daydreams –
when nature is viewed only through blue screens.

Anger steams off smeared floors and screens,
blocked friends, dismayed moms, teens remanded
after bullets rip schools, love *Never landed.*

Rufio hooks Peter on sports and computing.
I've seen lives reprogrammed in twelve steps,
joy in shucking the fake-self, no more phony schlep.

The Profit-Line Becomes the Priest
in the Cult of Never Enough
(Rachel) Carson was stunned by the lengths to which chemical companies would go to buy themselves a favourable public image. ~ Figuring, 436.

It's hopeless –
leaders make secret treaties
that exhaust and extract the hell
out of our planet and people;
when do the underpaid, reliant on food banks,
ever see their boss's promised pensions and jobs?

Do my taxes fund biased science,
masking DDT-clones sprayed worldwide,
heedless of biocide?

Allegiance
... the Thanksgiving Address, a river of words as old as the people themselves ...
~ Braiding Sweetgrass, 107.

Taught to salute the Flag, I'm impressed
by First People's Thanksgiving Address,
pledged, not to any nation, but to Nature –
naming all of creation every time.

They know loyalty to one nation
diminishes the rest, creates greed,
warrants wars, and relies on homilies
that goaded me: Do-good-works-or-fry-in-hell!

    May I pledge reverence
      that begets renewal

        and reciprocity –
    keeping Mother Earth alive.

Watery Dirge

Seas, your bed is dead-white, hosting no schools,
hearing no whales' mating search.

Urchins, sea grass, sand dollars, crabs and clams –
fried in a maelstrom they never sought.

My forebears built square-rigged ships
to rove Sail's Golden Age –
for distant novelties cravenly sought.

Whalers soon idled,
village-size cruise-ships storm ports –
tourists' holy grail of strange, now sought,

while starving and stateless refugees
fall to traffickers, desperately sought.

Lethal surges: resorts a barren Sahara,
pushed to the brink by us settlers, unsought,

       thinking: No, not us ...

Greta Thunberg
Swedish climate change activist, born in 2003.

Like evolved indigo children, Greta sounds the blues
over being sold the planet as candy store:
rain-forest lollipops, sugared soil, caramelized waters,
honeyed kangaroos, gummy bears.

She asks UN delegates: *Is this the world you give us?*

May Greta's voice carry sea to sea –
that her oceanic words pour balm
into beggars bowls, blackened breaths,
and quaking, flooded, parched escapees.

May she stop bottom-liners from mainlining profits.

May we refresh land and sea, sky and air –
rejoice in blue-jays, teal streams,
and forget-me-not blooms,
plant lilies in outmoded smokestacks,
     entice clear skies over
Beijing, London, New York, Toronto –
no pandemic with cancelled flights required.

Covid Correction

Mother Nature unwrinkles her brow,
cleansed of pesky jet contrails.

Cargo and cruise ships' scarcity unclogs
nature's veins of garroting particles,

waters, less bitingly torrid, regain
earth's AC rhythm: sea-cloud-rain-sea-cloud ...

Her desiccated, desertified quilts,
re-greened, cradle seed, feed and herbs.

But Covid is cruel – climate refugees and heroes
die beside eco-criminals.

The tipping point teeters on Covid's blood-red,
prickly surface, our wake-up shock,

admitted only in extremity.
We're cloistered –

our home exhales in relief.

Section III:

Holy In My Nature

Holy in My Nature

Ode to Parry Sound
(Seguin Township near Parry Sound, April, 1982 – April, 2023)

The well's thirsty, a first in thirty-six years,
yet Ontario boasts the most fresh water anywhere!

I beg the Goddess of Mercy, for rain –
despite a dry forecast, it does. A bit.

But the province is inflamed.
Again, northern reserves burn.
Again, First Nations must flee,
often as their water advisories.

Fear wildly on fire, I pack a getaway bag.
But I must leave my paintings.
And my appliances.

Will the Parry Sound Playland resemble
Dali's *"Beach Scene with Telephone"* dead zone?

What matters is clear as non-acidic rain:
without drinkable water, we die.
Desert women walk miles for this essential, daily.
To them, washing is sacred in its scarcity.

May the Great Spirit smother the fiery winds!

Mercy prevails – nearby fire snuffed out; I unpack.
Grateful for every drop; I've learned to conserve.

And face it, I live on favourable land.

Anatomy of a Wave

,.. bringing the sense of what was and of what is to come ... music ... that ... explodes against the rocks below ... ~ Rachel Carson, quoted in Figuring, 413.

The ocean speaks if I just listen
to its thunderous, sucking intake of breath.
Waves curl, crest and crash, heaving
an elegy – of life as I know it.

Boards glide on the concave, briny green,
attuned to the sudden snap.
Surfers become the combers' caretakers,
cringing at thoughtless humans
dumping sewage into crystalline waters.

Gulls squawk, eyeballing the banquet.

This roiling mirror is a sad reflection
of human neglect, no longer benign.

I gaze from the shore, transfixed.

Plastic glares back.

Cellular

Human life is an oceanic offering –
our primordial amoebic progenitor,
dwelling in our gut,
came to life to me long ago in grade school,
a visible thrill under a microscope;
its magnified wall pulsed like gills, lungs –
in-out, in-out, its own metronome.

And within its primal wall are the same
mitochondria that enliven my cells.

But Seventies shows: the *Bionic Woman,*
and the *Six Million Dollar Man,*
stoked the race for fake parts.

Versatile stem cells paled beside silicone.
Only the rich could augment their brains, beauty, brawn.

And now, Covid yearns to swim in our blood,
a swan song to healthy cells, with its narcissistic:
    O what a Big Bang am I.

Water Sign

For twenty years, I embraced Maritime crab trails,
                holy writ in sand.
Forty years in Lakeland, I splurged on Sobeys seafood,
                head office in Nova Scotia.

Smitten with clear oceans and briny scent,
                I dream crab habitats –
a vast lexicon of horseshoe and hermit,
                king and spider.

Why so enthralled with all things marine?
Because as a Cancer, I thrill
to the moon's pull in my blood.

The Algonquians also feel that tug,
singling out their moons: Strawberry, Harvest.

Intimately seasoned, this singularity
                begs us to drum
  to Luna's pulsing phosphorous
                and silver artistry,
rejoicing over her filigreed book of life,
                writ small.

Spindrift

Descended from sea captains and ship builders,
I'm part of the mystic, mercurial ocean.

    We can't use ocean as landfill or ignore
      the climatic, climactic Armageddon.

Plastic in my face, I decry my devolved usage –
glass to plastic, paper to plastic, oil to plastic ...

    Born before AI, bots, even television –
    I recall regattas of wind-whipped sailboats.

When waves spray my face, I romance schooners,
not TV's village-size, cruising *"Loveboat"*.

    It takes a village to provision
      –or evacuate –
        a cruise ship.

Unbroken

Dream met, Jack and I tour Hawaii's Big Island.
I swim, he sunbathes, both startled by a huge eel
chasing swimmers shouting to the heavens.

        God Kanaloa tends sea turtles,
            wild horses.

Car rentals too costly, we miss the famed waves,
huge hollow tubes surfers slide inside
that seeded my dreams before this marriage,

        unloved, drunk,
        and hollowed out.

I alone have fit lungs for high altitudes,
    touring Mona Kea by myself.
Respectfully, my guide stops below.

Volcano Goddess Pele's sacred summit.

Dizzy, I watch a sublime sunset fade,
in fifteen minutes, focus my eyes
on Pegasus and the Southern Cross.

        I know, solo or not,
           I am whole.

South Pacific and Mid-Atlantic

Hawaii promotes a romantic destination.
From a glass-sided sub off Kona, my spouse and I
submerge 100 feet below the colour red,
     into a blue-gold world:

  brain coral, angelfish, eel grass ...

But the seabed's tenements are broken;
Kahunas weep over their sacred turtles,
hugging the shore, not to lay eggs, but to die.
These priests' god, Kanaloa, howls. Why?

I mourn the damage done in a mere seventy years.

I toddled my first steps into the warm Atlantic,
    thrilled at this second skin.
  As a teen, I snorkelled in St. Thomas.

      From the sub, I surface,
     recall, eyes stinging
   under the sun's hotter glare.

Out of the Woods Yet
Paean to Creativity. The circumpolar Boreal Forest is the crown of the planet.
~ Arboretum Borealis, 1.

Forest deep where I dare to dream,
arty lines glisten in my gleam –
iambic, contour, melodic
lighting the trail to my hemlock.

My mate's ashes circle its bole
where I commune with long-dead souls.
That fragile and expressive line
joins me to red oak and white pine.

That visual, aural reprieve
weaves through welcoming leaves,
retrieves my awakened soul,
shimmies in nimbus, sears whole

my family's fragmented, snipped line –
art lengthened my aunt's timeline
but my parents and other kin
died young, no buffer given.

Forest deep where I dare to dream,
meter, gesture and trill redeem
the circling still-exiled hearts,
a full moon lightens these parts.

My seventy-plus years lock
on my life-dancing hemlock
absorbing my amorphous grief,
artful as sturdy burl, twirled leaf.

Death By Google

Half a continent away, I last saw you
at your dad's funeral.
Your niece emailed your passing.
I Googled your name. A thousand hits!

Diagnosed at Stage Three,
what time, what day, step-daughter?

        Years ago, you pointed out
      the surviving cedars, Seven Sisters.

Incomplete. Depleted.
I jogged my woods, a reminder
      of that stroll through Stanley Park,
      chickadees eating from our palms.

The Windfall Lake fire-pit jolted me.
Barb Tarbox's portrait glared on smokes:
This is how cancer death looks –
cigarette-thin, tendons strung out.
Never saw a pack on the fire-pit,

      never saw a smoke between your lips.

IT grad, you held tight your heart,
my grief's strength surprised me.
I felt the hurt your high IQ hid –

      the seven sisters, your aunts, far away.

Your niece replied – wrong name: you're alive!

Ontario, Fall 2017
(Died 16 February 2018)

To My Daughter
We exist in this moment of divinity, together. ~ Arboretum Borealis, 1.

Why do we inherit silverware, silky hair,
cold limbs, and prominent chins, but not
our elders' worldly won wisdom?

Letting go crowns an endless process
of disentangling miasma-bound mistakes,
owning our tortured tapestry.

Stark-sighted, I'm aware the muddy glue
is in me, not you. My own bogs beckon –
not those of your specific thickets.

My efforts to protect you fell way short.
My slow-grown *'Aha!'* arose
from marshy, red-faced sorrow.

Deep into motherhood, we choose
our stepping stones and sinkholes.

Nearing eighty, I'm blessed:
we thoroughly commune –
painting a new and dazzling tapestry.

It's No Hoax

Now deaths are part of the public airwaves,
mingling with stoked topics: Covid, Climate.

"Extreme weather events" normalize
hotter, colder, windier, wetter, drier hell –
despite the denials of those against hard facts.

How do you breathe air hot as 50 Celsius.

Where is the heart to choose what you value
when orders to flee hover in the flaming skies
thundering toward you?

Grass, flowers, rivers,
wildlife withdraw into themselves
at this murder of the temperate West Coast.

Stepping into the firewall is an outrage
equal to that of risking 50 below.

How many homes, hospices, fertile farms
are sacrificed to our hotheaded wants?

We will all join climate refugees,
robbed or killed or saved en route – to where?

Checking on friends
stuck on land's fragile front lines,
could you save the horses;
could you save your son's wheelchair?

Natural Divinity

Like the wind, you, Goddess, are revealed
      by Your ruffled impact –
opening the door for the woman with a walker;
    singing your praise to a child;
still giving love, despite its dismissal.

Breezes, cooling scorched words and gardens,
resemble Truth and Beauty holding hands
      around a Greek faience;
or warm-milk kindness heartening
      Bethlehem's beast.

God, infinitely beyond the limiting
Gender, Dogma, or Doctrine.

Your wind rustles my hair,
blackberries glow on a bush,
and blooms return
after Gypsy moth mayhem.

Scaling Down
Perhaps middle age is ... a period of shedding shells ... of ambition ... material possessions ... ego. ~ Anne Morrow Lindbergh, Gift from the Sea, (1955), 38.

After painting a never-ending nautilus:
each room, warm beige or gentle lilac,
I display my nature and water portraits.

My left-hand's crab-scrawled poems
gloss both the dark and the light.

Playing jazz on my whale-heavy piano,
I'm transported to tropical sea turtles.

Scaling back to a portable-life, still,
I keep piano and books; their shining pages
binding me to a pearl of eras, roles, styles, thoughts.

Right-sizing my ego's jellyfish stings,
no stellar starfish or formidable shark,
I free-style in the middle: one of a school,

or Cancer's crab, at times resistant
as cycles of continuous change

refine my character.

Harmony
And it seems to me, separated from my own species, that I was nearer to others.
~ Gift From the Sea, 15.

I sipped ginger-root tea on my twilit porch.
The setting sun slowed colour, sound, motion.

A full-stop allowed my absorption of a gift:
two groups of chickadees chorused
in the Burning Bush, the first flock
sounded a third higher than the second.

Communing they dispersed, still in harmony
and still in their separate sets.

I parsed what the two distinct pitches conveyed:
A message to me or a Birdland barbershop duet?

My tea tasted zestier, squares more chocolate.
The chickadees choraled an evening jazz, steamy, sweet.

So much I don't know, humans' eons ago
lost the ability to talk with trees. And birds.

What would we say to one another?
My petulant: Love your sound but not at 5am;
countered by your desperate:
Stop stealing my nesting space.

Solitude
*What a commentary on our civilization when being alone is suspect ~ **Gift from The Sea**, 20.*

The sand-crab trails, delicately silent,
are effaced by the next wave.

Each wispy line spools a love note,
tracing my thoughts out of self,
free of barnacled ego.

The elements converse – their language
subdues my sapiens squawk
that drowns out nearby birdsong.

Still, I'm enfolded in a sand-crab calm,
accounted for in this forever, forever fleeting.

Snug in my solitude, only half-clued in High Tech,
so far, I've held off the shrill siren
of digital society's pervasive invasion.

I've got time to luxuriate in sea and shore
while sea and shore remain on my watch.

Fledging

Each summer, the olive Flycatchers nested
over the porch's defunct light
to fledge two sets of babies.

The crested male flicked his tail,
flitted around the Burning Bush
or onto the Petunias, warning my cat and me:
Scram, this is my turf.

But I loved following his family antics,
and Henry drooled, Food.

Observing the clamouring tiny beaks
compensated for the cascade of droppings
spotting the wall and porch chair.

But after a deep scrub,
I noticed the nest empty.
No second birthing?

I left their nursery untouched.
Just in case ...

Once moved, on my vibrant balcony,
an olive Flycatcher enthralled Henry and me
every evening at dusk.

A southern feathered cousin?

Expansion

Underlying this stolen and spoiled land that shames me,
the news of sick water, dying herds and poisoned people
in crowded houses, is pushed underground.

If breached, the dilbit's slithering cylinder
rapes the land, paralleling the Highway of Tears
marking the breached, missing and murdered women
memorialized in an exhibit of moccasins that stunned me,
hundreds of souls crying out in the holy space.

Snaking through the sacred Sitka spruce,
Douglas fir, and Tlingit, Cree ... the Trans Mountain
bores through the miles high Rockies,
whose immensity led me to sobriety,
hailed invincible, but likely to leak into waterways.

If extended to the BC coast, unsuspecting
Haida natives and whales could inhale
oily waters, their lungs and gills gone grey,
soil seeping the black bleed and heated seed.

The black queen is ticked as her essence sucks out
and into the serpentine beast.
The pipeline mocks peace and the talking stick.

Protest signs become boardroom tables,
and the blockaders are jailed
in our woefully broken system.

Naming

Lost souls wail, wandering in empty ether,
finally heard, finally broadcast ...
clamouring in the moccasin exhibit
that smacked me into tears,
souls that join the missing, murdered women.

Children are ripped from loved ones,
schooled in a white culture's god, whose proxies
rubbed their privates, lashed their backs,
trained them to lower caste jobs.
Culture whipped out of them, they're made to pray
in an alien tongue to this white god –
that strikes terror if they slip up
far worse than that god's mild *Thou Shalt Not* ...
in the Sunday School I was made to attend.

Murdered by overlords for God and country
that ignored Indigenous burial rites.
Too many beloved sons and daughters
were stuffed into mass, unmarked graves.
A peacekeeper nation, accused of genocide,
called them savages! A country I chose
over my USA birthplace, equally culpable.

I beg my white culture that we bow down,
lose arrogance to become right sized,
and acknowledge our inhumanity,
driven by hatred and hubris, fear and folly.
No more twisted words,
let the mouldering truth be heard
to allow restoration.

Lost souls wail, wandering in empty ether,
overwhelmed by tears, needing to be named
and properly laid to rest, guided by Elders.

And in so doing, heal our climate, culture, country.

To Be a Bay
Only 30 percent of English words are verbs, but in Potawatomi that proportion is 70 percent. A bay is a noun only if the water is <u>dead.</u> When bay is a noun, it is defined by humans. ~ Braiding Sweetgrass, 53 and 55.

Imagine a language that allows a bay to be a bay,
not just a lump on a map,

but a nonhuman person

singing to cumulus and conversing with mergansers.

Georgian Bay is more than a biosphere
designating at-risk species, she was my home
for 40 years, a residence,
housing not just cottages stuffed with objects,
but also pike, pickerel weed, snappers, swimmers.

The English language reflects our obsession
with things, as if naming controls their nature.

In Potawatomi, things are named nouns
only if separated from living beings.

A basket, woven from black ash and sweetgrass,
reminded me they walk together, chemical-free.

This living art held blueberries and pinecones,
gifts gracing Georgian shores – and my trail
hugging Lake Ontario in St. Catharines.

Henry's Guests

In our former home,
my imposing Maine Coon Cat, Henry,
strolled inside with a playmate.

Not another chipmunk!
Cutely elegant, but what would this one chew?

Chippy One ate my Cheerios trail to the porch.
My waning sense of smell obscured
Number Two's exit, but a drop of blood
near Henry's litter disproved the tale
that cats don't eat chipmunks.

Chippy Three avoided me for days.
Finally, a sighting. I stepped on his (or her)
fluffy appendage before he'd flee,
and picked him up by that tail,
braving a bite? Rabies?

While crooning: I just want you outside,
I plopped him onto the porch. No chomp!

Stroking his quivering back: *There, there,*
I was stunned, neither of us harmed.
Did he sense my bare hands lifted him with love,
or was escape his primal thought?

Chipmunks can't climb up to my new balcony,
five flights up, but a flycatcher
obsessed Henry for hours.

Fortunately, my cat didn't jump!

Labyrinth

The silence between meals mellowed my marrow
at the women's retreat, a smile sufficing
when passing another pilgrim.

I did walk the Stations of the Cross
in this Jesuit-run solitude,
but my idea of Holy is many sourced –
singing bowl, birdsong, smudged four directions.

Spirit led me here, the labyrinth
a series of rings looping close
and far from centre, mirroring
my spiritual moods.

Suffused in sunshine,
a thought took residence in my mind,

      "I am well pleased,"

convincing me, my passage is on track.

    Now, over forty years demon-free,
I host that thought when life's a troubled maze;
    my feet circle to that sacred centre.

Blessings for my Grandchild

May you juggle joy like water
laughing over landscape,
may you stream outward kindly tributaries,
may you unearth your artistic self
buried in adolescent caves,
may you witness stars rising
in oceanic light shows,
may you attract starfish
shining your self-hood on shore,
may you enliven your soul
with a sunbeam's nutrients,
may you absorb the peace
of a star's immortal glow,
may you shimmer into friendship
like sea-grass sashaying to tides,
may you code an ode to yourself
like hermit crabs' flowing designs.

Love always,
Grandma

Nature Sings, Listen

Kate Marshall Flaherty's prompt: the poem "Can You Hear It?" by Paula Gordon Lepp.

Years ago, Ottawa's street sounds stunned me.
That ice storm performed malignant melodies:
trees' forlorn knocks, shaking on their feet,
ice-wires' zing, giving up ghostly voices.

Then at home, I heard crickets' joy: We're here!
blended to woodpeckers' Morse code messages.
Wish I could have heard robins slurping earthworms,
trout lilies waving freckled faces.

Such music in my former woods,
frogs did a quick surface-dive, plink, plink,
tree toads chorused: Peep, peep, peep, Spring!

Wish I'd heard daffodils' unfurling swish
as they threw showy heads at the sky
before moving to a city gifting me gardens galore.

Yes, I sleep in, no rising robin,
and I miss sunbeams' brush-stroked sky art.
And yet on my new balcony – I cup the moon in my hand;
it pours its light on my song-filled head.

BURNING UP #1
To Fossil Fuellers, Cronies, We Gas-fuelled Drivers
Someone in Gen Z easily has 60 years ahead; they'll live through the worst of Canada's forecast climate tolls. The average Canadian oil and gas executive is 58; the average federal MP, 50. "Canada in 2060," Anne Shibata Casselman, Maclean's, September 2023, page 39.

Do we want our grandchildren
witnessing their homesteads
     dissolving before their eyes
          windows crackling into glass missiles
               roof caving, car and driveway buckling
                   faded photos and love letters cindering
          baby shoes and trophies smouldering
     entire loved histories aflame?

Do we want our descendants
subsisting, bleak-eyed, doom-filled:
     witnessing blackened greenbelts
          drowning in the decimation of species
               gasping as homes slide into sea and swamp
               joining hoards of typhoon-fleeing homeless
          fighting each other for the last fish fillet
becoming the paranoid alt-right?

But Oil Suits, subsidies and profits
prop up your gilt-edged lifestyles; you can't resist:
     scorning us grannies chained to old growth
          slamming pipelines through sacred grounds
               squelching the true toxicity of your actions –
               don't you see: the boy with your brown eyes
          and girl with her ungovernable, curly mop
     deserve to breathe, eat, drink and sleep safely?

Don't you want your heirs to have a wall to hang?

BURNING UP #2
Can We Put the Fire Out?

Why does the Pacific plastic island vastly dwarf Lytton, B.C.?
The international inferno is Lytton,
the town that flamed into nada, nothing. RIP, 2021.

Now we're pouring accelerant
onto an overheated planet
where fires devour cars and condos,
cornfields and cougars,
as if the globe's one big campground bonfire.

Once-healthy hikes dance us into cancer,
sequoia and cedar crackle into charred tombstones,
caring-communities flare into bare ash,
flora and fauna fade into soon-to-be-fossils.

Haven't we pioneered solutions right now,
at least to lessen the ferocity
all-consuming winds, floods, fires –

allowing every being on earth
the slight odds of survival?

BURNING UP #3
Combustible Legacy

Oil moguls greenwash their greenhouse gases
and we still gas up at the pump, the propane tank.

Oil and gas execs hide their political bribes.
Huge gassy handouts increase their slick tricks:
heat-domes and porous pipelines
that jail us indoors or force us on the run,
even embryos can't escape the embroilment.

Air currents exponentially up the death toll,
        showering toxins
on those who never birthed them
    yet are the most brutalized.

Do we really want to bequeath our descendants
        a monstrous fiery pyre?

BURNING UP #4
Don't Bet on It

Jeff Bezos' and Richard Branson's new toys
shoot people into space
for a $250K per 10-minute romp,
rocketing oil fields' and oil rigs' worth in fuel
      into the air we inhale
           the water we swallow
                and the food we ingest.

Only millionaires and billionaires can afford
this astronomical, consequential whimsy.

Tied to earth, the rest of us pollute
      on highways
           heated buildings
               massive farms.

Billions of hungry poor tiptoe scant earthly imprints,
bare footprints trudging to
      waterholes
           tiny gardens
               small chicken coops
                    if they are lucky.

When fossil fuels burn through
        gated communities
           rentals and hovels
                street grates and shelters
           do we gamble on an invite
    to a habitable place in space?

BURNING UP #5
Wild Prayer

Ignored Mother Tree,
survivor of razed old growth,
slashing the status quo,
would you claim anything less
is but a murky oil slick trickling down
and messing with your mycorrhizal network
that keeps us breathing.

Reverence inhaled,
I listen, hugging the hemlock
for rooted messaging: what warnings
would they whisper to humanity?

Would the fading forest
call us on being embedded in the oil patch
and province of plastic,
plundering all that's healthy?

    How do we heal? Let's gaze at the place
where Stanley Park's Seven Sisters once stood;
        comprised of majestic Douglas Fir
          and Western Red Cedar
        cut down in the 1950's.

Their long-ago magnitude trims our egos,
        inspiring active prayers:
        serving in soup kitchens,
training as tree guardian firefighters,
        hopping onto bicycles –
spinning alternatives to gas and plastic.

BURNING UP #6
Our Grievous Embrace

We humans hug our only home's heart,
squeeze its breath, suck it dry –
lop our behemoths into logs,
split into dinettes and double beds.

Farmland bleeds the same crop,
replanted till the soil yawns,
fecund loam long gone.

Thwarted rivers impede the salmon's
dance to mate and spawn.

And we break and enter wildlife dens,
supplanting their highways with ours,
plus gas-breathing cars.

And we flail as earth out-flames other orbs,
burning up over our oily addictions.

This embrace smothers our Mother,
too weak to care for her children.

We bemoan our unrequited love.

Holy in My Nature

BURNING UP #7
Why Do Whales Wail?
Inspired by Johnson Cheu's "Wail"

For the young who ask
why whales wail, stymied by icebergs in sweltering waters.
We sing, glad for each rescue.

Infinite reasons I could give
why fissures crackle the heart.
We sing, glad love is our Gorilla Glue.

Your question arises
how light enters the *darkened pupil.*
We sing, glad for your youthful point of view.

Coiffed news anchors
need to speak the unspeakable, dear inspired teens.
We sing, sad that the wound in them is the wound in you.

Something smashed down, or welled up,
is the truth-seeking voice opening *outward,*
riding the bandwidths of active reconciliation.
We sing, glad ice clears a path for Beluga and Blue.

Love ought not to be
drowned in wounded blood,
but worn on sleeves for all to see.
We sing, glad Greenpeace ensures whales' wide purview.

The wound is within
the whales' warning wail
to restore our tortured planet. Now.
We sing, glad we'll wail into being –

a world where all creatures chorus
a Glad-to-be-Alive tune.

    And mean it.

BURNING UP #8
Fiery Pyre

In '82, I witnessed six stores flare up in our two-storey town –
 flames high as skyscrapers.
Five shops were restored, the Book Worm became earthworms.

Now in '23, fire eats kilometres for breakfast,
gallops over waterways, snacks on forests,
leaving bears charred or raiding backyards.

Fire speaks:
The god who fed and heated hominids with flames –
but without mercy or heart, I'm a serial killer
gobbling towns, businesses, homes, havens, habitats.

I cyclone into heat-domes –
air that's lost its way, molecules boiling over,
sucking lungs, gills and phloem inside out.
My flaming middle finger chastens humanity:

You in cahoots, you want hot, I give you hot,
burning alive land stewards, elephants,
fish three kilometres deep.

Worshippers of petrol, plastic, propane, who count
on shedding Earth to wreck another orb,
I give you white-hot particles
re-mapping your poor planet.

Pathetic humanity, pass the piping hot peppers,
dance till disbelievers char into ash.
Not six, but billions of trees and species join
Tyrannosaurus Rex and the Spirit Parade.

Or – we settle:
conflagration to campfire to candle flame –
lower our heads, revere the tiny light,
reset to our natural right size.

Honourable Harvest
Never take the first plant you find, as it might be the last – and you want that first one to speak well of you to others of her kind. ~ Braiding Sweetgrass, 182.

How do I escape the system of dominion
over the nonhuman, and heart-trust?

They feed, cure, and house all, teaching reciprocity.
My former forest taught me to hope.

I trekked to a hillside flush with plump, green leaves,
trillium trumpeting wild leek season.

The first two ramps resisted, replying:
No to the permission I sought.
So, I harvested only three per patch.

Those thick-stemmed, big bulbs mellowed
my seafood and veggie medleys;
their leaves peppered my salads.

Grateful for this bounty, I mothered my haven.
Mindful of ironwood's life-pulse, I chanted:
Save this tree, this forest, this planet;
a prayer that moved with me
to the garden city.

But it's all in the respect –
thinking leek, pine, and toad,
or mulberry, catalpa, and squirrel,
as he or she, not as it,
takes time,

time to soften but activate my footstep,
what's in my vision to insure there are still
trees to breathe, soil to flower, water to float life.

Testimonials

What if they organized an apocalypse and nobody cared? That horrific, real-time truth is what Katerina Fretwell contests in Holy in My Nature. These are EMERGENCY poems: Crack the spine and dial 911. But only if you treasure an animal's "lope" over the "trophy" of its head on a killer's wall; only if you realize that you are not just "reading Dante," but now must truly "live the Inferno, / die in one of the subterranean rings." Despite the bitter fact of "we humans squandering our heirloom / As if chopping up inherited antiques," Fretwell presents these urgent meditations as lyric elegies, summoning us to action.~ **George Elliott Clarke, Author of "Canticles III (MMXXIII)" & Parliamentary Poet Laureate of Canada (2016 & 17)**

Fretwell takes up Greta Thunberg's challenge of "Is this the world that you leave us?" in a cascade of sorrows, eulogies, nostalgias, landfills, clear-cuts, prayers, warnings, rebuffs, satires and sacred curses, all swept into an anthem of resistance and hope for her grandchild.
~ Harold Rhenisch, author of "The Salmon Shanties".

These poems testify to the "climate carnage" we have been perpetrating. At first glance, the "I" can be associated with the poet, but the speaker frequently slips in and out of this mask. The "I" is not omniscient but learning and unlearning. In some poems, the speaker altogether fades into the imagery. We are left with nature uninterrupted by human consciousness. Still, in others, the use of personal pronouns invites us to acknowledge the presence of nature in ourselves. Confronting these pronoun shifts, the reader may ask, "Who is speaking? Is it me, or is it you? What is this about? Is it about them or about us?" ~ **Bänoo Zan, author of "Letters to My Father"**

ENDNOTES

Weapons of Mass Revelation: The title comes from Sophie Hackett's "Far and Near: New Views on the Anthropocene," in *Anthropocene,* edited by Edward Burtynsky, Jennifer Baichwal and Nick de Pencier, Goose Lane, (2018) 13 – 33.

***Personal Anthropocene:* Solastalgia**, coined by Australian Glenn Albrecht: grief at what's already lost from environmental change.

Phosphate Mining, Lakeland Florida: Aired on CBC, WWF warned of 68% average species loss.

Micro Burst – *Plastics Primer:* The poem was inspired by Conor Mihel's article, "Drowning in Plastic," *Ontario Nature,* Spring 2019,

A (Re)Use for Everything: Inspired by Johanna Silver, "Mission Possible," *Living,* July/August 2019, 52-53.

Primeval: Inspired by Peter Kuitenbrouer, "Pine Solved," *The Walrus*, May 2019, 24 – 25.

Ode to Parry Sound: Salvadore Dali's "Beach Scene with Telephone, 1938, foreshadowed WW2.

Natural Divinity: Faience: funeral urn.

Acknowledgements:

Poems in *Holy in My Nature* have appeared in anthologies: *Dancing on Stones*, editor John Di Leonardo, *Sage-ing #30*, *Love Lies Bleeding*, editor George Elliott Clarke, *Cannery Row*, editors John Jantunen and Tanja Rabe; *By the Wishing Tree*, editor Becky Alexander. *Community Poetry Anthology*, editors Vanessa Shields and Irene Moore Davis; *Heartwood*, editor Lesley Strutt. Penn Kemp's *River Revery* online; *League of Canadian Poets Poetry Pause*. Thanks to Sandra Harris, We 4 and Niagara Writers Groups, StillPoint Prompts and Editing Circles, Penn Kemp, Susan McCaslin, Peter Midgley and George Elliott Clarke for their continued support.

Publishing history: Monographs: Poetry Books:
We Are Malala, Inanna, 2019; *Dancing on a Pin*, Inanna, 2015. Long-listed for Lowther prize, in IFOA's Battle of Bards, 2016; listed in Michael Dennis's poetry blog, five poems Runner Up, *subTerrain*, Outsider; *Class Acts*, Inanna, 2013. Listed in Kerry Clare's Best Poetry Books of 2013, 49th Shelf, and a poem from *Class Acts* was a finalist in *Descant's* Winston Collins Poetry Prize, 2012; *Angelic Scintillations*, Inanna, 2011; *Shaking Hands with the Night*, Pendas Productions, 2008; *Samsara: Canadian in Asia*, Pendas Productions, 2004; *Remyth*, Cranberry Tree Press, 1997, as Kathy Fretwell; *Apple, Worm and All*, Fiddlehead Poetry Books, 1979, as Kathy Tyler; *The Ultimate Contact*, Fiddlehead Poetry Books, 1977, as Kathy Tyler.

Anthologies:
Intimate Passages, [compiler and illustrator], The Ontario Poetry Society, 2020; *The Eloquent She: Arms Like Ladders*, [editor and illustrator], LCP Feminist Caucus, 2006; *And no one knows the blood we share*, [editor], LCP Feminist Caucus, 2005; *Mix Six: Six Ontario Poets*, [contributor] Mekler and Deahl, 1996.

Journals:
Prism international, Descant, The Capilano Review, subTerrain Magazine, Room, Quarry, Vallum, Scrivener, The Fiddlehead, Bogg, Welsh *Scintilla #16* and *#17, Rampike* and *Dry Wells in India, Crossing Lines: Poets who came to Canada during the Vietnam War, Close to the Heart, Poets in Response to Peril, Quartzite Dialogues* poem sequence, set to music and performed at *The Festival of the Sound*, 1999, 2004, 2014, and *Takefu Music Centre*, Tokyo, 1999.

Author Profile

Katerina Fretwell is a poet and visual artist. Her most recent solo art show was at Gallery 814, Toronto, ON 2018; She won First Prize for Watercolour, Artfocus group show, Toronto 2001; and her art resides in Copenhagen, Tokyo, Toronto and across Canada and the US. She's travelled through Asia, Europe, North and Central America and concludes she has lived in some of the world's most stunning areas. She is aware of so many extinctions and extreme weather events and strives to commemorate flora and fauna in her poems and paintings.

Since moving to Seguin Township, Ontario in 1982, Katerina has noticed a huge decline in wildlife in the woods in the area. A former Maritimer, born in the water sign of Cancer, she loves all things oceanic. She is a former competitive swimmer and loved swimming in Rankin Lake, before moving to St. Catharines, the garden city, to be close to family.

www.ingramcontent.com/pod-product-compliance
Lightning Source LLC
Chambersburg PA
CBHW060032040426
42333CB00042B/2404